Spectacular Sports

Rodeo

Counting

Joseph Otterman

Consultants

Colene Van Brunt
Math Coach
Hillsborough County Public Schools

Publishing Credits

Rachelle Cracchiolo, M.S.Ed., *Publisher*
Conni Medina, M.A.Ed., *Managing Editor*
Dona Herweck Rice, *Series Developer*
Emily R. Smith, M.A.Ed., *Series Developer*
Diana Kenney, M.A.Ed., NBCT, *Content Director*
June Kikuchi, *Content Director*
Susan Daddis, M.A.Ed., *Editor*
Karen Malaska, M.Ed., *Editor*
Kevin Panter, *Senior Graphic Designer*

Image Credits: front cover, p.1 Jo Crebbin/Shutterstock; pp.4–5 Mlenny/iStock; p.5 (bottom) Jesse Beals/ Icon SMI/Corbis via Getty Images; pp.6–7 Woodkern/iStock; p.9 Granger Academic; p.10 (bottom) Library of Congress [loc.gov/pictures/resource/highsm.36252/]; p.12 Alison Scott/Corbis via Getty Images; p.13 Kokoulina/Shutterstock; p.14 Scott Olson/Getty Images; p.15 Lincoln Rogers/Shutterstock; p.17 (top) Kobby Dagan/VWPics/Alamy Stock Photo; p.18 photo-denver/Shutterstock; p.19 (bottom) Jason Connolly/AFP/Getty Images; all other images from iStock and/or Shutterstock.

Library of Congress Cataloging-in-Publication Data

Names: Otterman, Joseph, 1964- author.
Title: Spectacular sports : rodeo / Joseph Otterman.
Description: Huntington Beach, CA : Teacher Created Materials, [2018] | Includes index. | Audience: K to Grade 3. |
Identifiers: LCCN 2017054932 (print) | LCCN 2018008035 (ebook) | ISBN 9781480759701 (eBook) | ISBN 9781425856762 (pbk.)
Subjects: LCSH: Rodeos for children--Juvenile literature. | Counting--Juvenile literature.
Classification: LCC GV1834.4 (ebook) | LCC GV1834.4 .O88 2018 (print) | DDC 791.8/4--dc23
LC record available at https://lccn.loc.gov/2017054932

Teacher Created Materials
5301 Oceanus Drive
Huntington Beach, CA 92649-1030
www.tcmpub.com

ISBN 978-1-4258-5676-2

Printed by: 51497
Printed in: China

Table of Contents

What Is It?

What has clowns, horses, and tricks but is not a circus?

It is a rodeo!

Two cowboys ride their horses.

Rodeo clowns perform for the crowd.

A rodeo is a type of **contest**. Cowboys and cowgirls show their **skills**. They try to be the best.

A cowgirl makes a hard turn around a barrel.

Let's Do Math!

There were 47 cowboys and cowgirls at the rodeo last year. There are 62 this year. Count from 47 to 62 on the hundreds chart.

1	2	3	4	5	6	7	8	9	10
11	12	13	14	15	16	17	18	19	20
21	22	23	24	25	26	27	28	29	30
31	32	33	34	35	36	37	38	39	40
41	42	43	44	45	46	47	48	49	50
51	52	53	54	55	56	57	58	59	60
61	62	63	64	65	66	67	68	69	70
71	72	73	74	75	76	77	78	79	80
81	82	83	84	85	86	87	88	89	90
91	92	93	94	95	96	97	98	99	100

How Rodeo Began

Most sports start for fun. But rodeo got its start with work.

These cowboys try to catch this calf using a lasso, or rope.

These cowboys catch a bull on a ranch.

This cowboy wrestles a bull.

These cowboys catch a bull.

Cowboys and cowgirls met to work in the fields.

They wanted to find out who had the best skills.

A young cowgirl shows off her lasso skills.

This cowboy is happy after winning a bull-riding contest.

They had contests to find out! In time, the contests turned into rodeos.

Let's Do Math!

The best cowboys and cowgirls win a prize. A **belt buckle** is a common prize.

1. How many belt buckles are there?

2. What number is 1 less than the number of belt buckles?

3. What number is 1 more than the number of belt buckles?

Animals

Animals are part of rodeos. People ride them.

Some horses **buck**. It is hard for the rider to stay on.

This cowgirl holds on tight.

Staying on a bucking horse is hard.

Cattle are part of rodeos, too. Cowboys and cowgirls ride them. They may **rope** them as well.

Two cowgirls work together to rope a bull.

Riding a bull takes skill.

Yee-haw!

There is no sport quite like rodeo. It is a lot of fun! It is exciting, too!

This cowboy wears gear to stay safe.

This cowgirl shows her riding skills.

Problem Solving

The rodeo is a busy place! There is so much to see.

What You See	Numerals	Clues
cowboy hats		1 less than 49
horses		1 more than 15
ropes		1 less than 80

1. Write numerals for what you see at the rodeo using the clues.

2. Choose two things from the table. Show how many there are using pictures or objects.

Glossary

belt buckle—metal piece that attaches two ends of a belt

buck—to jump and bolt violently

cattle—all types of cows, bulls, and steers

contest—competition to see who is best

rope—to capture using a rope

skills—abilities people have from training and practice

Index

Answer Key

Let's Do Math!

page 7:

47, 48, 49, 50, 51, 52, 53, 54, 55, 56, 57, 58, 59, 60, 61, 62

page 13:

1. 21 buckles
2. 20
3. 22

Problem Solving

1. 48
   16
   79
2. Pictures or objects will vary but should represent 48, 16, or 79.